D0929141

SandCastle 3

Homophones

You're On Your Phone

Mary Elizabeth Salzmann

ABDO
Publishing Company

Published by SandCastle™, an imprint of ABDO Publishing Company, 4940 Viking Drive, Edina, Minnesota 55435.

Cover and interior photo credits: Comstock, Rubberball Productions, Stockbyte

Library of Congress Cataloging-in-Publication Data

Salzmann, Mary Elizabeth, 1968-
    You're on your phone / Mary Elizabeth Salzmann.
        p. cm. -- (Homophones)
    Includes index.
    Summary: Photographs and simple text introduce homophones, words that sound alike but are spelled differently and have different meanings.
    ISBN 1-57765-797-7
    1. English language--Homonyms--Juvenile literature. [1. English language--Homonyms.]
I. Title. II. Series.

PE1595 .S295 2002
428.1--dc21

                                                                                    2001053308

The SandCastle concept, content, and reading method have been reviewed and approved by a national advisory board including literacy specialists, librarians, elementary school teachers, early childhood education professionals, and parents.

Let Us Know

After reading the book, SandCastle would like you to tell us your stories about reading. What is your favorite page? Was there something hard that you needed help with? Share the ups and downs of learning to read. We want to hear from you! To get posted on the ABDO Publishing Company Web site, send us email at:

sandcastle@abdopub.com

About SandCastle™
Nonfiction books for the beginning reader

- Basic concepts of phonics are incorporated with integrated language methods of reading instruction. Most words are short, and phrases, letter sounds, and word sounds are repeated.

- Book levels are based on the ATOS™ for Books formula. Other considerations for readability include the number of words in each sentence, the number of characters in each word, and word lists based on curriculum frameworks.

- Full-color photography reinforces word meanings and concepts.

- "Words I Can Read" list at the end of each book teaches basic elements of grammar, helps the reader recognize the words in the text, and builds vocabulary.

- Reading levels are indicated by the number of flags on the castle.

SandCastle uses the following definitions for this series:

- Homographs: words that are spelled the same but sound different and have different meanings. *Easy memory tip: "-graph"= same look*

- Homonyms: words that are spelled and sound the same but have different meanings. *Easy memory tip: "-nym"= same name*

- Homophones: words that sound alike but are spelled differently and have different meanings. *Easy memory tip: "-phone"= sound alike*

Look for more SandCastle books in these three reading levels:

Level 1 (one flag)	Level 2 (two flags)	Level 3 (three flags)

Grades Pre-K to K 5 or fewer words per page	**Grades K to 1** 5 to 10 words per page	**Grades 1 to 2** 10 to 15 words per page

you're

you are

your

belonging to you

Homophones are words that sound alike but are spelled differently and have different meanings.

You're coming over to my house.

I am watching for **your** car.

Flying a kite is fun.

I am holding the string and **you're** holding the tail.

Good for you.

You caught a fish on **your** hook.

You're just in time for my tea party.

Do you like milk in **your** tea?

You're using a bucket to lift your things into the tree house.

This is a fun ride.

You're making it go very fast.

I am almost done.

Then it will be **your** turn.

Your doghouse is finished.

Now **you're** going to stay dry when it rains.

We have neat costumes.

I am a clown and **you're** a ghost.

We are working together.

I am pulling the wagon and **you're** pushing it.

Your yellow pail makes great sand towers.

May I use it next?

We are racing across the field.

You're about to catch up to me.

You're having a bath.

Soon **your** fur will be shiny and clean.

I like **your** birdhouse.

You're almost done putting on the roof.

Our outfits are almost the same.

I am wearing pink and **you're** wearing blue.

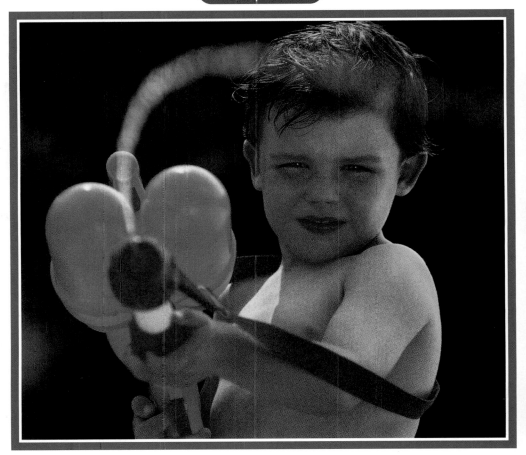

What will happen to **your** clothes if I spray you?

(They will get wet.)

Words I Can Read

Nouns
A noun is a person, place, or thing

bath (BATH) p. 18
birdhouse
(BURD-houss) p. 19
blue (BLOO) p. 20
bucket (BUH-kit) p. 10
car (KAR) p. 6
clothes (KLOHZ) p. 21
clown (KLOUN) p. 14
costumes
(KOSS-toomz) p. 14
doghouse
(DAWG-houss) p. 13
field (FEELD) p. 17
fish (FISH) p. 8
fur (FUR) p. 18

ghost (GOHST) p. 14
homophones
(HOME-uh-fonez)
p. 5
hook (HUK) p. 8
house (HOUSS) p. 6
kite (KITE) p. 7
meanings (MEE-ningz)
p. 5
milk (MILK) p. 9
outfits (OUT-fitss) p. 20
pail (PAYL) p. 16
pink (PINGK) p. 20
ride (RIDE) p. 11
roof (ROOF) p. 19

sand (SAND) p. 16
string (STRING) p. 7
tail (TAYL) p. 7
tea (TEE) p. 9
tea party
(TEE PAR-tee) p. 9
things (THINGZ) p. 10
time (TIME) p. 9
towers (TOU-urz) p. 16
tree house
(TREE HOUSS) p. 10
turn (TURN) p. 12
wagon (WAG-uhn) p. 15
words (WURDZ) p. 5

Pronouns
A pronoun is a word that replaces a noun

I (EYE) pp. 6, 7, 12, 14,
15, 16, 19, 20, 21
it (IT)
pp. 11, 12, 13, 15, 16

me (MEE) p. 17
they (THAY) p. 21
this (THISS) p. 11
we (WEE) pp. 14, 15, 17

what (WUHT) p. 21
you (YOO)
pp. 4, 8, 9, 21

Verbs

A verb is an action or being word

am (AM)
　　pp. 6, 7, 12, 14, 15, 20
are (AR)
　　pp. 4, 5, 15, 17, 20
be (BEE) pp. 12, 18
belonging
　　(bi-LONG-ing) p. 4
catch (KACH) p. 17
caught (KAWT) p. 8
coming (KUHM-ing)
　　p. 6
do (DOO) p. 9
done (DUHN) pp. 12, 19
finished (FIN-isht) p. 13
flying (FLYE-ing) p. 7
get (GET) p. 21
go (GOH) p. 11

going (GOH-ing) p. 13
happen (HAP-uhn)
　　p. 21
have (HAV) pp. 5, 14
having (HAV-ing) p. 18
holding (HOHLD-ing)
　　p. 7
is (IZ) pp. 7, 11, 13
lift (LIFT) p. 10
like (LIKE) pp. 9, 19
makes (MAKESS) p. 16
making (MAKE-ing)
　　p. 11
may (MAY) p. 16
pulling (PUL-ing) p. 15
pushing (PUSH-ing)
　　p. 15

putting (PUT-ing) p. 19
racing (RAYSS-ing)
　　p. 17
rains (RAYNZ) p. 13
sound (SOUND) p. 5
spelled (SPELD) p. 5
spray (SPRAY) p. 21
stay (STAY) p. 13
use (YOOZ) p. 16
using (YOOZ-ing) p. 10
watching (WOCH-ing)
　　p. 6
wearing (WAIR-ing)
　　p. 20
will (WIL) pp. 12, 18, 21
working (WURK-ing)
　　p. 15

Adjectives

An adjective describes something

alike (uh-LIKE) p. 5
clean (KLEEN) p. 18
different (DIF-ur-uhnt)
　　p. 5
dry (DRYE) p. 13
fast (FAST) p. 11

fun (FUHN) pp. 7, 11
good (GUD) p. 8
great (GRAYT) p. 16
my (MYE) pp. 6, 9
neat (NEET) p. 14
our (OUR) p. 20

same (SAYM) p. 20
shiny (SHINE-ee) p. 18
wet (WET) p. 21
yellow (YEL-oh) p. 16
your (YUR) pp. 4, 6, 8, 9,
　　10, 12, 13, 16, 18, 19, 21

Adverbs

An adverb tells how, when, or where something happens

about (uh-BOUT) p. 17
almost (AWL-most)
  pp. 12, 19, 20
differently
  (DIF-ur-uhnt-lee) p. 5
just (JUHST) p. 9

next (NEKST) p. 16
now (NOU) p. 13
on (ON) p. 19
over (OH-vur) p. 6
soon (SOON) p. 18
then (THEN) p. 12

together
  (tuh-GETH-ur) p. 15
up (UHP) p. 17
very (VER-ee) p. 11

Contractions

A contraction is two words combined with an apostrophe

you're (YUR) pp. 4, 6, 7,
  9, 10, 11, 13, 14, 15, 17,
  18, 19, 20